PRIMARY SOURCES OF
FAMOUS PEOPLE IN AMERICAN HISTORY™

NATHAN HALE

HERO OF THE AMERICAN REVOLUTION

JODY LIBERTSON

rosen central
Primary Source™

The Rosen Publishing Group, Inc., New York

Published in 2004 by The Rosen Publishing Group, Inc.
29 East 21st Street, New York, NY 10010

Library of Congress Cataloging-in-Publication Data

Libertson, Jody.
Nathan Hale: hero of the American Revolution / by Jody Libertson.—1st ed.
    p. cm. — (Primary Sources of Famous people in American history)
Summary: Surveys the life of Nathan Hale, a Revolutionary War hero whose service to George Washington as a spy cost him his life.
Includes bibliographical references and index.
ISBN 0-8239-4117-5 (lib. bdg.)
ISBN 0-8239-4189-2 (pbk.)
6-pack ISBN 0-8239-4316-X
1. Hale, Nathan, 1755-1776—Juvenile literature. 2. United States—History—Revolution, 1775-1783—Secret service—Juvenile literature. 3. Spies—United States—Biography—Juvenile literature. 4. Soldiers—United States—Biography—Juvenile literature. [1. Hale, Nathan, 1755-1776. 2. Spies. 3. United States—History—Revolution, 1775-1783—Secret service.] I. Title. II. Series.
E280.H2L53 2004
973.3'85'092—dc21

                                                          2002155943
Manufactured in the United States of America

Photo credits: cover, pp.13, 23 © Bettmann/Corbis; pp. 4, 24 © Corbis; pp. 5, 9, 18, 19, 26 © North Wind Picture Archives; p. 7 courtesy, Rare Book Department, the Free Library of Philadelphia; p. 10 courtesy of the First Congregational Church of Coventry, 1171 Main Street, Coventry, Connecticut, gathered in 1712 (the Reverend Doctor Bruce J. Johnson); p. 11 © Lee Snider/Corbis; p. 15 National Archives and Records Administration; pp.16, 22 Picture Collection, the Branch Libraries, the New York Public Library, Astor, Lenox, and Tilden Foundations; p. 17 Library of Congress Geography and Map Division; p. 21 painting by R. Sterling Heraty, courtesy of the Antiquarian and Landmarks Society, Hartford, Connecticut; p. 25 State Historical Society of Missouri; p. 25 (inset) courtesy, Print Collection, Miriam and Ira D. Wallach Division of Art, Prints and Photographs, the New York Public Library, Astor, Lenox, and Tilden Foundations; p. 27 Collection of the New-York Historical Society, Negative Number 50381; p. 28 Adriana Skura; p. 29 © Farrell Grehan/Corbis.

Designer: Thomas Forget; Photo Researcher: Rebecca Anguin-Cohen

CONTENTS

CHAPTER 1	Growing Up in Connecticut	4
CHAPTER 2	From Teacher to Soldier	10
CHAPTER 3	Hale Becomes a Spy	16
CHAPTER 4	Hale Is Caught	20
CHAPTER 5	Hanged and Martyred	26
	Timeline	30
	Glossary	31
	Web Sites	31
	Primary Source Image List	31
	Index	32

1 GROWING UP IN CONNECTICUT

Nathan Hale was born on June 6, 1755, in Coventry, Connecticut. His father, Richard, was a farmer and a deacon. His mother, Elizabeth Strong, raised the children. Both of Nathan's parents were patriots. They believed that America should not be ruled by the British. Nathan had eight brothers and three sisters.

This eighteenth-century map shows the colony of Connecticut, where Nathan Hale grew up. Connecticut was mostly wilderness with some small towns and farms.

Hale became a captain in the army for American independence. He was just 21 years old. The American army was poorly trained. It had few supplies.

Nathan was often sick as a young boy. As he grew, he became strong and healthy. He enjoyed fishing, swimming, and wrestling. In school, Nathan liked to read about the heroes of history. The village minister, Reverend Joseph Huntington, helped him study for college.

NATHAN'S LOVE FOR READING

Nathan Hale loved to read as a child. Later, he became the librarian of a secret reading group at Yale University.

In colonial times, students used hornbooks (shown here). A hornbook was made of wood and looked like a paddle. Paper attached to the wood face was printed with the alphabet and numerals.

In 1769, Nathan went to Yale University in New Haven, Connecticut. He was a good student and read books on many subjects. He liked to give speeches and play sports. Nathan graduated college in 1773. He became a teacher in Connecticut. Students and their parents liked Nathan. He was friendly, honest, and trustworthy.

DID YOU KNOW?

At a town meeting, Hale gave a speech about liberty that impressed the crowd.

Shown here is a drawing of Yale University in the 1700s. The top students in the area studied here. Many studied for law practice. Nathan Hale wanted to teach children instead.

2 FROM TEACHER TO SOLDIER

Hale believed girls should learn the same subjects as boys. Most men of that time did not think that way. In April 1775, the American Revolution began. Hale was then teaching in New London, Connecticut. Like his family, Hale believed that the American colonies should be free from British rule.

Shown here is the First Congregational Church, where the Hale family worshiped. A monument to Nathan is in the cemetery of this church.

Nathan Hale's first teaching job was in this schoolhouse in East Haddam, Connecticut. In colonial times, all classes were taught in one or two rooms. Children of different ages were taught at the same time.

Hale enjoyed teaching. He thought that he had a duty to teach his students. He also felt that he should join the fight for American independence. On July 1, 1775, Hale became a lieutenant in the Continental army. Later, he fought in the attack of Boston. He showed that he was a brave soldier.

FIGHTING FOR LIBERTY

In April 1775, the Battle of Lexington started the Revolutionary War. Nathan Hale quickly joined the local military in New London, Connecticut.

This drawing shows the Boston Tea Party on December 16, 1773. Patriots dressed as Native Americans jumped onto British ships. They dumped all the tea into Boston Harbor.

People left Boston in March. They were afraid. On April 30, 1776, Hale moved to New York City to join the army there. In May, he and other soldiers captured a small British boat. It held useful supplies that the army needed. Hale became a captain of Knowlton's Rangers. The Rangers' job was to keep watch on the British in New York.

DID YOU KNOW?

In July 1776, the Declaration of Independence was agreed upon by the founding fathers.

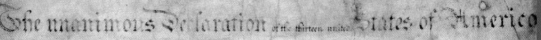

Thomas Jefferson wrote the first draft of the Declaration of Independence. It was signed by representatives from the thirteen colonies. It listed the political ideas that the colonies wanted to rule themselves by.

3 HALE BECOMES A SPY

In September 1776, General George Washington asked for an army captain to spy on the British. Washington needed to find out what the British were planning to do next. Hale was the only one who offered to do the job. He knew he would be killed if he were caught. He also knew spying could help win the war.

This drawing shows Hale getting his orders from General George Washington. Hale wanted to do something important for the revolution.

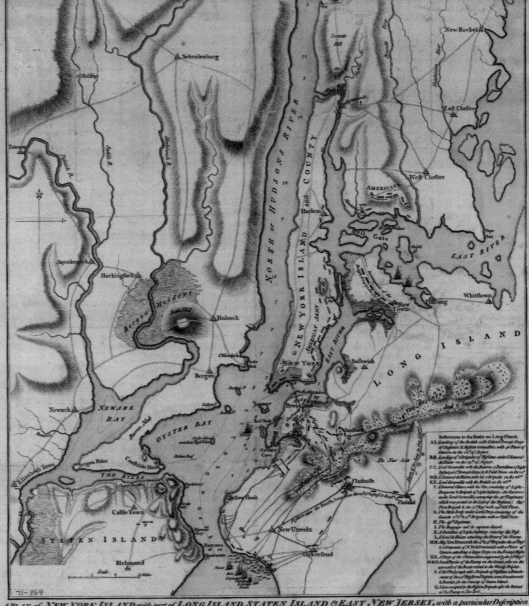

A PLAN of *NEW YORK ISLAND*, with part of *LONG ISLAND*, *STATEN ISLAND* & *EAST NEW JERSEY*, with a particular Description of the ENGAGEMENT on the Woody Heights of Long Island, between FLATBUSH and BROOKLYN, on the 27.th of August 1776. between *HIS MAJESTY'S FORCES* Commanded by General HOWE and the *AMERICANS* under Major General PUTNAM, with the subsequent Disposition of both ARMIES.

This is a map of New York and part of Long Island. American and British armies held land on either side of the East River. On September 16, 1776, Nathan Hale sneaked behind enemy lines on Long Island.

Hale's friend Captain William Hull tried to talk him out of becoming a spy. Hale told Hull that he wanted to be useful. Hale wanted to do something important for the war. On September 12, Hale went to the British camps on Long Island, New York. He pretended to be a schoolmaster. Inside the camps, he took notes on everything he saw and heard.

This picture shows the Battle of Long Island in August 1776. The British beat the Americans in this battle. American soldiers can be seen turning away from the battle.

Captain William Hull knew spying was dangerous. He was afraid for his friend. He knew the British might kill a spy they caught.

4 HALE IS CAUGHT

Hale learned important military facts from the British. He wrote down those facts on paper. This was not wise. If caught, the British would easily know he was a spy. Hale had not been prepared well to be a spy. His cover story as a schoolteacher was weak. The British could have easily found out who he really was.

THE MARK OF A SPY

Spies usually were people who fit easily in with a crowd. Hale was very tall. He also had blond hair. Hale stuck out in a crowd.

Shown here is a watercolor of Nathan Hale by R. Sterling Heraty. As a spy, Hale visited British camps on Long Island. He wrote notes in Latin and hid them in his shoes.

Hale left the British camps in late September. He carried his notes with him on his way back to General Washington. On September 21, Hale was captured before he could get back to New York. Some people think his Tory cousin, Samuel Hale, spotted him. He was taken to General Howe, the British army general.

This drawing shows how the British might have captured Nathan Hale. Hale was making his way back to Manhattan. British soldiers captured him before he could get back behind American lines.

General Sir William Howe (shown above) questioned Hale after his capture. Howe would not give Hale a trial. He wanted the young captain to die by hanging for his crime.

GEN. SIR WILLIAM HOWE

Howe ordered Hale to be executed the next day. Hale was not given a trial before he was hanged. The next morning, British army officer Captain John Montresor brought Hale into his office. Hale wrote one letter to his brother Enoch and one to Colonel Knowlton. Hale did not know that Colonel Knowlton had been killed in a battle.

General William Howe commanded the war from the Beekman Mansion. This house is located near present-day 51st Street and First Avenue in New York City. Nathan Hale wrote his last letters from a room in this house.

The inset painting shows British Captain John Montresor. Montresor told the only surviving eyewitness account of Hale's capture and execution to an American army captain, William Hull. In 1827 Hale's friend, Stephen Hempstead, wrote a letter to the *St. Louis Republican*. Hempstead told of his last meeting with Hale before his spy mission.

5   HANGED AND MARTYRED

Hale asked for a Bible before he was hanged. This was refused. Hale gave an important speech before he was executed. He ended the speech with the now famous line, "I only regret that I have but one life to lose for my country." Hale died on September 22, 1776, at the age of 21.

This drawing shows Nathan Hale just before his execution. Hale's request for a clergyman was turned down.

An article titled "Nathan Hale, the Patriot Spy" ran in the *New York Herald* on November 26, 1893. Hale was a powerful symbol of American patriotism.

It is unknown where Hale was buried. The American army learned later that Hale had been caught and hanged. His story was told throughout the colonies.

Hale became a hero for his actions. He was a hero like those he read about as a schoolboy. Hale was called a martyr because he gave up his life for his country.

This plaque hangs at Third Avenue and East 66th Street in New York City. Its location shows the most likely place where Hale was executed. Historian William Kelby determined this spot by using notes taken from a British officer.

This statue of Nathan Hale stands in City Hall Park in New York City.

TIMELINE

1755—Nathan Hale is born on June 6.

1769—Nathan Hale goes to Yale University in Connecticut.

1773—Nathan Hale graduates from Yale University.

1774—Nathan Hale accepts a teaching job in New London, Connecticut.

1775—The Battle of Lexington occurs, starting the Revolutionary War. Nathan Hale joins the army. He arrives in Boston.

1776—The Continental army leaves Boston to move to New York. Nathan Hale leaves shortly after.

1776—The Declaration of Independence is signed; Knowlton's Rangers is formed, and Nathan Hale joins.

1776—Nathan Hale accepts assignment as a spy and is hanged less than two weeks later.

GLOSSARY

Continental army (KON-tin-EN-tul AR-mee) The army created during the Revolutionary War.

deacon (DEE-kun) An officer of a church who helps with church duties.

evacuate (ee-VA-kyoo-ayt) To leave an area immediately because it is not safe.

execute (EK-suh-kyoot) To put to death.

liberty (LI-bur-tee) Freedom.

impressed (im-PREST) Made people aware of abilities through words and actions.

independence (in-dih-PEN-dents) Freedom.

lieutenant (loo-TEH-nent) An officer in the army.

martyr (MAR-ter) Someone who dies or is killed for a cause or a principle.

patriot (PAY-tree-uht) Someone who loves his or her country and is prepared to fight for it.

Tory (TOR-ee) A colonist who was loyal to the British government and wanted to remain under the rule of Britain.

trial (TRYL) When a case is decided in court.

WEB SITES

Due to the changing nature of Internet links, the Rosen Publishing Group, Inc., has developed an online list of Web sites related to the subject of this book. This site is updated regularly. Please use this link to access the list:

http://www.rosenlinks.com/fpah/nhal

PRIMARY SOURCE IMAGE LIST

Page 4: 1771 hand-drawn map of New England, by Carington Bowles.
Page 5: Hand-colored engraving of Captain Nathan Hale, published in *History of New York*, ed. James Grant Wilson, 1892.
Page 7: Photo of eighteenth-century hornbook. It is currently housed at the Free Library of Philadelphia.
Page 9: 1784 hand-colored woodcut of Yale College, New Haven, Connecticut.
Page 10: Circa 1880s photograph of First Congregational Church, Coventry, Connecticut. It is currently housed at the First Congregational Church, Coventry, Connecticut.
Page 11: A photograph by Lee Snider, circa 1980s, of the East Haddam, Connecticut, schoolhouse where Nathan Hale taught.
Page 13: *The Boston Tea Party*, a Currier & Ives colored lithograph.
Page 15: The Declaration of Independence, 1776. It is currently housed at the National Archives, Washington, D.C.

Page 16: *Hale Receives Instructions from Washington*, an 1880 print by Howard Pyle. It is currently housed at the New York Public Library, New York, New York.

Page 17: 1776 map of New York and Long Island, by Georges-Louis LeRouge. It is currently housed at the Library of Congress, Washington, D.C.

Page 18: Late eighteenth-century hand-colored engraving by James Smillie of the Battle of Long Island.

Page 19: Hand-colored portrait of William Hull, circa 1770s. It is currently housed at the Library of Congress, Washington, D.C.

Page 21: Undated watercolor of Nathan Hale by R. Sterling Heraty. It is currently housed at the Antiquarian and Landmarks Society, Hartford, Connecticut.

Page 22: *The Capture of Nathan Hale*, a late eighteenth-century print by William Henry Snyder. It is currently housed at the New York Public Library, New York, New York.

Page 23: 1777 illustrated portrait of General Sir William Howe.

Page 24: Undated engraving titled *The Old Beekman Mansion House, New York City*.

Page 25: Photographed copy of a page from the January 27, 1827, *St. Louis Republican*, showing a letter by Stephen Hempstead.

Page 26: Hand-colored woodcut engraving of Nathan Hale's execution, appearing in 1860 edition of *Harper's Weekly*.

Page 27: Photographed copy of a page from the November 26, 1893, edition of the *New York Herald*, showing the article "Nathan Hale, the Patriot Spy," written by William Kelby.

Page 28: Bronze memorial plaque of Nathan Hale noting the spot where Hale was probably hanged. It currently hangs on the wall of the Chatham apartment building at Third Avenue and East 66th Street, New York City.

Page 29: Farrel Grehan photograph of a statue of Nathan Hale, sculpted by Frederick MacMonnies. It now stands in City Hall Park in New York City.

INDEX

A
American Revolution, 10, 12, 14, 16-18, 20-24

B
Boston, 12, 14
Britain/the British, 4, 10, 14, 16, 18, 22

C
Connecticut, 4, 8, 10
Continental army, 12

E
execution, 24, 26, 28

F
famous speech, 26

H
Hale, Elizabeth Strong, 4
Hale, Enoch, 24
Hale, Richard, 4
Hale, Samuel, 22
Howe, William, 22
Hull, William, 18
Huntington, Joseph, 6

K
Knowlton, Thomas, 24
Knowlton's Rangers, 14

L
Long Island, New York, 18

M
Montresor, John, 24

N
New York City, 14

P
patriots, 4

S
spy, 16-18, 20-22

T
teaching, 8, 10, 12

W
Washington, George, 16, 22

Y
Yale University, 8

ABOUT THE AUTHOR

Jody Robertson is a writer and editor living in New York City.